EASTER ISLAND

Giant Stone Statues Tell of a Rich and Tragic Past

Text and photographs by Caroline Arnold

Clarion Books • New York

TITLE PAGE: *Half-buried statues on the slopes of Rano Raraku*

PAGES 2–3: *Ahu Tongariki, destroyed by a tidal wave on May 22, 1960, was recently restored.*

ADDITIONAL PHOTO AND ILLUSTRATION CREDITS
Arthur Arnold, pp. 19 (left), 34, 37 (top), NASA, p. 9,
Gloria and Jim Turner, pp. 28 (bottom), 29, 38 (bottom), 39,
Bishop Museum, Honolulu, Hawaii, p. 35.

ACKNOWLEDGMENTS
I would like to thank the following people for their help and inspiration: my daughter, Jennifer Arnold, and her husband, Humberto Gutiérrez-Rivas, for encouraging me to visit Chile and Easter Island; my husband, Arthur Arnold, and Gloria and Jim Turner for their help with photos; and the Fonck Museum in Viña del Mar, Chile.

Clarion Books
a Houghton Mifflin Company imprint
215 Park Avenue South, New York, NY 10003
Copyright © 2000 by Caroline Arnold.
The text for this book was set in 14-point Tiepolo Book
For information about permission to reproduce selections from this book, write to
Permissions, Houghton Mifflin Company, 215 Park Avenue South, New York, NY 10003.

Printed in Hong Kong.

Library of Congress Cataloging-in-Publication Data
Arnold, Caroline.
Easter Island : giant stone statues tell of a rich and tragic past / text and photographs by Caroline Arnold.
        p.   cm.
Includes bibliographical references and index.
Summary: Describes the formation, geography, ecology, and inhabitants of the isolated Easter Island in the Pacific Ocean.
ISBN 0-395-87609-5
1. Easter Island—History—Juvenile literature. 2. Easter Island—Antiquities—Juvenile literature.
[1. Easter Island.] I. Title.
F3169.A76 2000
996.1'8—dc21   99-27189
        CIP
SCP 10 9 8 7 6 ·5 4 3 2 1

CONTENTS
CONTENTS

Island in the Middle of the Sea

Sixteen centuries ago, in about A.D. 400, a small group of seafarers and their families sailed east across the Pacific from their island homes in central Polynesia. Their large double canoes were filled with food, water, tools, and other things they needed to survive. After many weeks they reached the rocky shores of a small island, later known as Easter Island. There they established homes, planted gardens, and started a new life. They developed a rich and complex culture that lasted for more than a thousand years. Perhaps their most remarkable and unique accomplishment was the carving of giant stone statues called *moai*. They created nearly a thousand of these stone figures, some more than three stories high, and erected hundreds of them on huge stone altars called *ahu*. Even more amazing is that all this was accomplished by people whose only tools were stone, bone, and coral.

The first European visitor to Easter Island was a Dutch sea captain, Jacob Roggeveen, who landed there on April 5, 1722. In the tradition of his time, he named his "discovery" for the day of his arrival, which was Easter Sunday. Today the island is known both as Easter Island (Isla de Pascua in Spanish) and Rapa Nui, a Polynesian name given to it in the nineteenth century by Tahitian sailors. Both the people and the traditional Easter Island language are known today as Rapanui.

Moai at Tahai, on Easter Island's west coast

Toppled moai are testimony to Easter Island's violent past.

At the time of Roggeveen's arrival, Easter Island was no longer the paradise it had once been. The land had been stripped of its forests, food was in short supply, and families were at war with one another. During the next century and a half, the situation only grew worse. By 1888, when the government of Chile took over Easter Island, all of the *moai* had been toppled from their *ahu,* and the majority of the native population had died in brutal clan wars, in violent encounters with outsiders, or from starvation and epidemic disease. On an island that had once supported a population of four thousand or perhaps many more, only a few hundred people remained. Their descendants are among the people who live on Easter Island today. Although they remember and continue some of the old traditions, many details of the island's past have been lost or forgotten.

Our knowledge of Easter Island's history comes from reports of early visitors, from information conveyed in family histories and traditional tales, and from studies of the ruins and other ancient remains on the island. Besides the giant *moai,* the evidence includes the remains of houses, fire pits, garden enclosures and other structures, stone and bone tools, drawings on rocks, carved wooden

View from the crater Puna Pau. Now, as in ancient times, much of Easter Island's land is tilled for agriculture.

figures, and panels covered with a kind of picture writing known as *rongorongo*.

The first systematic studies of Easter Island's ancient history were conducted by Katherine Routledge, an Englishwoman who spent seventeen months on the island in 1914 and 1915. In 1935, much of the island was designated as a national park to protect the ruins. Father Sebastian Englert, a Catholic priest who lived on Easter Island from 1935 to 1969, made the first complete survey of the statue platforms, and he recorded stories and memories of the older inhabitants. Many other researchers, including the American archeologist William Mulloy, who came with Thor Heyerdahl's expedition in 1955, have also made important contributions to our understanding of Easter Island's past. Today, ancient sites continue to be excavated and, in some cases, restored. Modern scientific techniques are being used to learn more about Easter Island's human and natural history. Among the many questions still being asked are: Who were the first settlers? Where did they come from? How did they live? How and why did they construct such giant statues? And, perhaps most important, what caused the end of this once thriving community?

Easter Island is the most isolated inhabited place on earth. It is a tiny speck of land with a total area of just sixty-four square miles—an area about the same size as Washington, D.C. Located in the Pacific Ocean five hundred miles south of the Tropic of Capricorn, Easter Island is two thousand two hundred miles from the South American coast to the east, and one thousand four hundred miles from even tinier Pitcairn Island, the closest populated land to the west. In view of Easter Island's size and the vastness of the surrounding ocean, it is amazing that it was ever discovered at all.

Easter Island is the easternmost corner of the large triangle of Pacific Islands known as Polynesia. The other corners are formed by the Hawaiian Islands to the north and New Zealand to the west. Because Easter Island is south of the tropics, its climate varies with the seasons. Summer, which begins in December, tends to be warm and dry, whereas winter weather is somewhat cooler and rainier.

Easter Island was formed when three large volcanoes erupted from the sea floor. Their peaks form the corners of this triangle-shaped land. Rano Aroi, on the north coast, is the tallest and most recent volcano, having erupted about a million years ago. Rano Kau, in the southwest, is the site of the ceremonial village of Orongo. Rano Raraku, which contains the quarry where most of the giant statues were carved, is a secondary cone of the larger volcano Maunga Terevaka, on the eastern tip of the island. None of the Easter Island volcanoes have erupted since people began to live there.

When the first human settlers arrived on Easter Island, the vegetation looked very different from what we see today. Thick forests of both hardwoods and palm trees covered much of the island. This began to change as people cleared the land to make fields for planting and cut down trees to provide firewood and lumber and, in later times, to make devices for moving the giant statues. By the time the first Europeans came to Easter Island, it was a bare, treeless land. Today, parts of the island have been reforested, but the main impression is of an open, grassy landscape.

ABOVE: *Inside the crater of the volcano Rano Kau is a deep freshwater lake. Rano is the Rapanui word for a crater.*

BELOW LEFT: *Polynesia*

BELOW RIGHT: *Easter Island viewed from space. The crater of Rano Kau is visible on the lower left.*

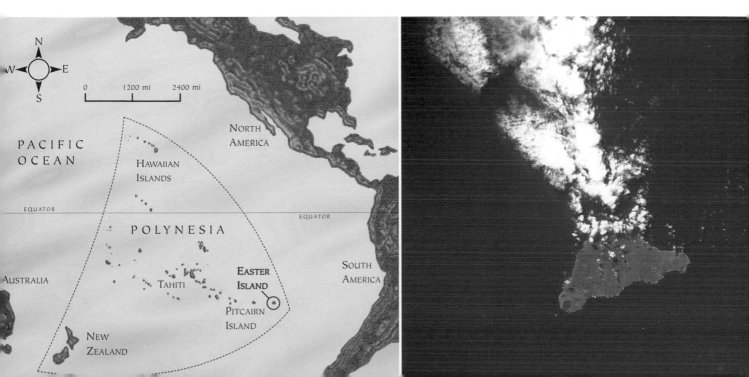

THE FIRST SETTLERS

Exploration of the South Pacific islands began more than three thousand years ago, when people originally from New Guinea settled the islands of Tonga and Samoa. The customs and traditions developed there were the beginning of Polynesian culture. By 300 B.C., or possibly earlier, these Polynesian seafarers began to explore and settle islands much farther to the east. For these journeys they may have taken advantage of the shift of winds that occurs periodically during El Niño years.

Traveling in long canoes lashed together for stability in the open ocean, the Polynesian explorers carried with them plants, animals, and other supplies needed to settle a new land. These expert navigators were skilled at finding their way across the sea by using the sun and stars as a kind of sky map. They also had a keen understanding of the movement of wind and waves. Clues to land ahead included observations of the flight paths of land-dwelling birds as they returned to their roosts in the evening, changes in wave patterns, certain kinds of cloud formations that clustered over land, and plants floating in the water.

Most experts believe that Easter Island was settled by Polynesians, possibly sailing from the Marquesas Islands, and that they arrived about A.D. 400. Both the physical traits of the people on Easter Island and their customs and traditions are similar to those found elsewhere in Polynesia. In 1774, when Captain James Cook visited the islands, a Tahitian man on his ship was able to speak with the Easter Islanders because of the similarity between their language and his own.

Many people wonder whether Polynesians ever sailed to the South American coast or whether South Americans ever sailed to Polynesia. It is certainly possible that people could have made this journey, as the Norwegian explorer Thor Heyerdahl demonstrated when he sailed his boat, the *Kon-Tiki*, from Peru to Polynesia in 1947. However, there is no proof that South Americans ever traveled to Easter Island in ancient times.

Thor Heyerdahl spent much of his life trying to show a connection between the traditions of Easter Island and the art and customs of western South America to support his belief that the first settlers of Easter Island were South Americans. Although most experts today do not think that this was likely, Thor Heyerdahl did stimulate much popular interest in Easter Island through the books he wrote about his adventures. He also made many important discoveries during his visits to the island.

Opposite above: A cave where people lived at Tahai. The heaviest settlement of Easter Island was near the coast.

Below left: A rocky coast makes the landing of boats on Easter Island treacherous.

Below right: Banana trees were among the many plants brought to Easter Island from Polynesia.

The Legend of Hotu Matu'a

According to tradition, the first settlers of Easter Island were the great navigator and Polynesian king, Hotu Matu'a, and his large family. Although details of Hotu Matu'a's story vary among sources, historical and archeological evidence corresponds with much of the legend.

Soon after Hotu Matu'a's arrival, family members dispersed across the island, eventually forming eight separate family groups, each with its own name and territory. Then, sometime after they were settled, tradition says, another group arrived. The new group, all men, were large and more heavyset than the original settlers. They also practiced the custom of elongating their earlobes. This was done by piercing the ear and gradually enlarging the hole. In many translations of the story the newcomers are referred to as the Long Ears, as opposed to the Short Ears, or original settlers, even though the Rapanui words describing the new arrivals, *Hanau Eepe*, may actually mean "heavyset people." In later times, the practice of elongating the ears spread throughout the community and may have been a mark of class distinction.

As on many other islands in Polynesia, Easter Island society was an aristocratic one, with an upper class and a working class. Some family groups had higher status than others. Families also sometimes formed alliances with one another. Within each kin group there were warriors, priests, craftsmen, farmers, and fishermen. The highest-ranking individuals of the community were the priests, who were known as *ariki*. The supreme religious leader on the island was the *ariki henua*. Although the *ariki henua* did not rule in a political sense, the power that he embodied was important for ensuring the health and welfare of the entire island. In Polynesian society the role of *ariki henua* is typically passed from father to son. Hotu Matu'a was the first in a long line of *ariki henua* on Easter Island.

Moai at Anakena. Hotu Matu'a is said to have landed at Anakena, the only sandy beach on the island.

One ancient name for Easter Island was Te Pito Te Henua, Rapanui words meaning the "navel, or center, of the world" or possibly "land's end." These round stones on the island's north coast are believed to represent the center of the world.

DAILY LIFE

Except when they slept or took refuge from bad weather, the ancient Rapanui people spent most of their time outdoors. The simplest and most common shelters were caves. (The Rapanui word for cave is *ana*.) Caves are numerous in the volcanic rock of Easter Island and include long underground passageways that were created during the formation of the island as flowing lava cooled and hardened. Caves continue to form along the coastline as ocean waves erode the rock at the water's edge. During periods of civil unrest and the slave raids of the 1800s, caves with secret entrances provided places where people could hide.

People also constructed houses of stone on the island. These varied from small round houses for a single family to large buildings meant for dozens of people. People built walls by piling stones on top of one another, and although no mortar was used to hold them together, the walls were quite sturdy.

In many places on the island there are stone foundations that resemble the outline of a boat or canoe. They were for a type of house called a *hare paenga*. (The Rapanui word for house is *hare*.) *Hare paenga* are believed to have been reserved for priests or other high-ranking men in the community. It is said that Hotu Matu'a slept in a *hare paenga*. Near Anakena there are remains of one that is 160 feet long, certainly a dwelling of royal proportions. In front of the entrance to the *hare paenga* there was usually a semicircular stone patio where people met to work, eat, or talk.

Many of the *hare paenga* foundation stones have holes drilled in them to hold wooden poles. The poles were arched across the foundation to form supports for the long horizontal bars to which thatch was tied. The thatch was made of rushes, or stems, of the *totora* plant, which grew in the shallow water at the edges of the crater lakes. *Totora* reeds were also used for weaving baskets and mats, and were bound together to make small surfboard-like swimming rafts.

ABOVE LEFT: *Model of a hare paenga covered with thatch. The shape of the house resembles an overturned canoe. The single entrance almost always faced the sea.*

ABOVE RIGHT: *Stone foundation of a hare paenga*

BELOW: *Totora reeds growing in the crater lake of Rano Raraku. Pollen grains accumulated in the sediment at the bottom of the lake provide a record of ancient plant life on the island.*

LEFT: *Sugar cane. Recent studies of ancient skeletons show that many people suffered from an unexpectedly high level of tooth decay, possibly a result of eating so many sweet foods.*

RIGHT: *Yams were a staple of the Easter Island diet.*

The Easter Island settlers brought with them a variety of seeds and plants. Many of these crops, including bananas, sugar cane, sweet potatoes, yams, and taro root (a starch), are still grown today on the island. Settlers also brought paper mulberry trees, a plant whose bark could be pounded to make a kind of cloth.

The main clothing for men was a loincloth; women wore a kind of skirt or apron. High-ranking chiefs sometimes wore capes that were often dyed yellow or orange. People also wore a variety of hats, both on ceremonial occasions and as a reflection of rank or an indication of their mood. Early visitors also noted that people decorated their bodies with elaborate painted or tattooed designs.

The settlers needed to plant gardens because the natural resources of the island did not include a wide variety of edible plants. The main food-producing plants were tall palm trees. Caches of petrified palm nuts discovered in Easter Island caves show that the trees provided food for early settlers. A similar palm species, the Chilean wine palm, which grows in South America today, produces nuts as well as sap that can be used for making sugar, syrup, and wine.

LEFT: *Earth ovens were sometimes marked by a rectangle of stones on the surface of the ground.*

RIGHT: *Large stone bowls, called taheta, are often seen near home sites and were used to collect rainwater for drinking.*

In prehistoric times on Easter Island, food was usually cooked in stone-lined pits, or earth ovens, called *umu*. The stones were heated by burning a wood fire over them. Then the fire was removed, and food wrapped in wet mats or leaves was placed on top of the hot stones. Dirt was mounded over the pit, and the heated stones cooked the food. The process could take several hours, depending on the kind and quantity of food being cooked.

All living things, including wood that is burned to make charcoal, contain carbon. Because carbon atoms change at a regular rate, scientists can analyze them to determine age of an object. Charcoal found in ancient fire pits on Easter Island can be used to establish the time when that pit was used.

There is no permanent source of fresh water on the surface of Easter Island except for the crater lakes. Both now and in prehistoric times, farmers have depended on rain to water their crops. In some places along the coast, archeologists have found large basins, or reservoirs, that were dug in ancient times, apparently to collect rainwater. Islanders also sometimes built stone walls around their gardens both to protect the plants from the drying effect of wind and to keep water from draining away.

One of the ways that we learn about how people lived in the past is to look at what they threw away. Over time trash accumulates in layers, with oldest items located at the bottom. Animal bones, discarded after a meal and preserved in middens, or trash piles, tell us about the kinds of meat that Easter Islanders ate.

The only domestic animals that were kept on the island were chickens. Dogs also came with the early settlers but did not survive. Chickens were an important source of food and were also valued as items for gift exchanges and as religious offerings. Rats, which came as stowaways in the canoes, were occasionally eaten as well. For other sources of protein the islanders had to depend on native birds and sealife.

Because of Easter Island's location south of the tropics, the water is too cold for most corals to grow, and there is no surrounding reef. Thus, fish that thrive in the protected waters of a reef are not as plentiful on Easter Island as in warmer parts of Polynesia, and they were less important as a food source. Nevertheless, Easter Islanders did eat fish, which they caught both from shore and from boats. They also harvested shellfish in shallow water.

Easter Island fishermen caught fish by hand as well as with nets, spears, and hooked lines. Fishhooks were made from both stone and bone. In some cases, after a great fisherman died, fishhooks were carved from his bones. It

LEFT: *Jacob Roggeveen and other eighteenth- and nineteenth-century visitors to Easter Island commented on the abundance of chickens.*

RIGHT: *At night, chickens were placed inside enclosures like this to prevent them from being stolen.*

was believed that his bones continued to hold the power and good luck of his fishing ability.

When excavators studied trash heaps from the early years of settlement, they were surprised to discover that nearly one third of all animal bones were from porpoises. Perhaps these large sea mammals were a substitute for fish in the diet. Most likely people harpooned the porpoises at sea from large canoes. When excavators searched layers representing periods after 1500, they found no more porpoise bones. By that time, most of Easter Island's large trees, which were necessary to make oceangoing canoes, had been cut down. With no boats, deep-sea fishing and porpoise hunting would no longer have been possible. At this time, most land birds, which depended on forests for food and places to nest, also disappeared from the Easter Island diet. Instead, chickens began to play a much larger role as a food item. By the end of the seventeenth century, human bones began to appear in trash heaps as well, as cannibalism became more common. Ritual cannibalism in the aftermath of war had long been a part of Easter Island tradition and was an act of insult by the victors toward the conquered. Cannibal meals were usually only for military chiefs and their warriors, but the practice may have spread during periods of widespread food shortages.

LEFT: *Stone fishhooks show the steps of the carving process.*

RIGHT: *Fishermen launched their canoes into the sea from ramps like this one.*

STONE ALTARS

STONE ALTARS

Besides basic supplies for survival, the settlers of Easter Island brought with them from central Polynesia many ideas, customs, and religious practices. These included the construction of large outdoor altars, or *ahu*. It was not until the later years of settlement that Easter Islanders began to place large statues on some of the *ahu*.

There are more than 245 *ahu* on Easter Island, and in most cases they are located close to the shore. Spaced an average of a half-mile apart, they form an almost unbroken ring around the island. Each *ahu* belonged to a family group and is located on the territory where that family or clan lived. The *ahu* may have been used to mark the boundaries between family properties. Some *ahu* appear to be large altars where religious ceremonies were performed. Others were built as burial chambers. Some may have been used for both purposes.

A typical *ahu* is constructed from carefully worked slabs of stone that form the top and outer walls. Some of these facing stones weigh as much as seven tons. They are supported by rubble or rough-cut stones in the middle of the *ahu*. Because the *ahu* were often rebuilt, this fill sometimes included broken statues or the remains of an older structure. The seaward-facing wall of the *ahu* is often quite steep, while there is usually a gently sloping ramp leading to the *ahu*'s landward side. In front of many *ahu* there is a kind of plaza created by a pavement of round stones set into the ground.

Most *ahu* were built parallel to the shoreline, but a few face other directions. Of these, more than half point toward the rising or setting sun either at the equinox (when day and night are equal) or at the solstices (which mark the longest and shortest days of the year). Experts think these *ahu* may have been used as solar calendars. For people who depended on nature for their livelihood, it was important to know about the changing seasons. Farmers needed this information to determine the best time for planting. A knowledge of the seasons may have helped the people plan for the arrival of migrating birds, fish, and turtles—animals that they caught seasonally for food. The position of the sun could also have helped fishermen and other navigators find their direction when going out to sea.

The seaward wall of the ahu at Tepeu is of particularly sturdy construction.

The most spectacular *ahu* of all are those that were built to support *moai*, the huge stone figures that are unique to Easter Island. Although large statues were carved on other Polynesian islands, on none of those are sculptures as huge or as numerous. Some of the Easter Island *ahu*, one of which is nearly two hundred yards long, support as many as fifteen statues in a long line. Other *ahu* have only a single figure. Most *moai* face away from the sea.

The *moai* were venerated and believed to possess powers, but they were not representations of deities. According to tradition, each *moai* represents an ancestor of the family or clan. They are known generally as *aringa ora*, which means "living faces."

Moai at Ahu Tongariki

Although Easter Islanders carved some stone images during their early years on the island, the creation of monumental figures did not begin until they had been there for several hundred years. The earliest-known statue mounted on an *ahu* is the sixteen-foot-tall *moai* located just north of Tahai. It was made in the twelfth century. The last *moai* to be mounted on a platform is at Hanga Kioe and was placed there about 1650.

Sizes of *moai* vary greatly. Some are as short as six feet, but the usual size is between eighteen and twenty-three feet tall. In general, the smaller *moai* represent early periods of carving, while the bigger *moai* are the most recent. The largest *moai* ever placed on an *ahu* was the thirty-two-foot giant at Ahu Te Pito Kura. It is estimated to weigh eighty-two tons. The tallest *moai* ever carved remains in the quarry, still attached to its base. That statue is sixty-five feet long and may weigh up to 270 tons!

The body shapes of the *moai* vary as well. Some are short and compact. The medium-size *moai* either have straight cylindrical bodies or triangular-shaped bodies with wide shoulders and narrow hips. The largest *moai*, including those still in the quarry, all have straight, slender bodies.

BELOW: *Moai at Tahai represent several sizes and body shapes.*
OPPOSITE: *Tahai. The weathered moai in the foreground is the oldest known moai to be erected on an ahu.*

Making the Moai

Most of the more than nine hundred Easter Island *moai* were carved from the walls of the volcano Rano Raraku. They are made of tuff, or hardened volcanic ash, a stone that is relatively soft and easy to carve. About fifty of the *moai* were carved from other materials found elsewhere on the island. Some were made of a dark red volcanic stone called scoria. A few of the *moai* were carved from basalt, a tough, fine-grained stone that is created when lava solidifies slowly. Basalt can be ground and polished to a fine, smooth surface.

Sometime in the late 1600s, before the arrival of the first Europeans, the carving of the *moai* came to an abrupt halt. Half-finished *moai* were abandoned in the Rano Raraku quarry, while others were left on the lower slopes of the mountain or alongside roads on their way to an *ahu*. Nearly four hundred statues remain at the quarry in various states of completion. They provide clues to the process of statue making.

The completion of a single *moai* was a long, slow process. When Thor Heyerdahl visited Easter Island in the 1950s, he hired a team of six men to make a statue using ancient stone tools. They quit after three days, but based on their progress, it was calculated that six men working every day could complete a large statue in twelve to fifteen months.

The ancient Easter Island statue makers were skilled craftsmen specially trained in the art of stone carving. They were privileged and honored members of the community, and according to legend, they did no other work. They were provided with food by fishermen and farmers. Ruins of stone houses found at Rano Raraku are believed to be the places where the sculptors lived.

Sculptors carved the *moai* with *toki*, adzes, or axlike tools, made of basalt. Thousands of *toki* litter the ground in the Rano Raraku quarry. Basalt was also used to make axes for wood cutting as well as fish hooks and household tools. Obsidian, a glasslike rock that is formed when lava cools rapidly, is another stone that Easter Islanders used for tools. Obsidian is extremely hard and can be shaped into a razor-sharp cutting edge. It was used to make cutting and scraping tools, drills, and files. A piece of obsidian absorbs tiny amounts of water when it is cut, so the age of a tool can be determined by the quantity of water that has been absorbed at its cut edges.

OPPOSITE ABOVE: *The quarry at Rano Raraku*
BELOW: *Basalt and obsidian tools*

Sculptors carved a *moai* with the statue lying on its back. After chipping the outline of the statue's profile into the quarry wall, they made a niche around it so they could work from both sides. People at the back side worked in a cramped space about two feet wide and five feet deep. The sculptors began by carving the head of the *moai* and finished with the hips.

No two *moai* are exactly alike, although most follow a basic model. All of them are designed to be standing figures with the base at about hip level. The arms hang straight down the side of the body, but the hands, which have elongated fingers, curve around the front of the abdomen. *Moai* heads are elongated and always face forward. Most of the faces have narrow lips, large noses, and deep eye sockets below a large forehead. The ears are usually long and sometimes have depressions in the earlobes where ornaments could be inserted.

Finished statues were polished with pieces of coral to produce a smooth, shiny surface. In some cases the *moai* bodies were engraved with elaborate designs, which are believed to represent tattoos. Most of the *moai* are male, although there are a few examples of female figures.

OPPOSITE ABOVE: Moai in its niche in the quarry

OPPOSITE BELOW: Ahu Nau Nau at Anakena

RIGHT: Designs carved on the moai's back represent tattoos and the belt of a ceremonial loincloth.

Moving the Moai

After the carving of the top, or the front half, of the *moai* had been completed, the bottom was slowly undercut until only a narrow ridge of rock attached it to the quarry. This ridge was then cut away, and the *moai* was lowered to the bottom of the hill with ropes. There the figure was set upright into a hole in the ground, and the carving of the back was finished. The standing statues that now litter the slopes of Rano Raraku are abandoned *moai* whose lower portions gradually became buried by eroding rocks and soil from above.

The real challenge in moving a finished *moai* was getting it from the quarry to the *ahu* where it would be erected. Most of these sites were at least several miles away, an enormous distance to transport a huge object weighing many tons. The ruts of several roads that were used for moving statues to various parts of the island from the quarry can still be seen.

No one knows exactly how the *moai* were moved or whether the statues were transported lying down or standing up. A variety of experiments have been conducted to test possible methods of

transportation, both with real *moai* during the process of reconstruction and with models.

Some experts think that a *moai* was fastened onto a wooden sledge and pulled to an *ahu*. A system of logs used as rollers may have made the task easier. Mashed yams or other plant material might have been used to make the path slippery. In the 1950s, Thor Heyerdahl organized a group of about 180 people to pull a thirteen-foot statue fastened to a wooden sledge. They easily pulled it a short distance, proving that this method could have been used in ancient times. Another theory is that statues were moved forward with a system of levers and pulleys.

When a statue finally reached the *ahu*, it would have been gradually raised on a ramp and tipped into place. In some cases, stones were wedged around the statue's base to help make it level. Traces of color on some of the *moai* suggest that the statues may have been painted after they were raised.

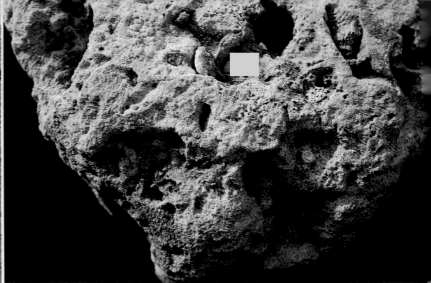

Topknots and Eyes

Between fifty and seventy-five of the *moai* on Easter Island once wore cylindrical hatlike blocks of red stone, called *pukao*, on their heads. The *pukao* were quarried from red volcanic stone found in the crater of the volcano Puna Pau. A large cylinder was cut from the quarry, then rolled to the *ahu*, where the carving was completed. No one knows whether the *pukao* was placed on the *moai*'s head before or after the statue was mounted on the *ahu*.

When placed on the head of a *moai*, a *pukao* gave the statue extra height and grandeur. It may have served to distinguish a *moai* from others without such decoration, or to indicate that different kinds of rituals should be performed at these *ahu*. Many experts believe that the *pukao* were meant to look like hair wound into a topknot or wrapped in a kind of turban. Others suggest that they might be hats or feathered crowns.

Many of the *moai* have indented eye sockets with a small ledge for a piece of coral. A circle of darker stone in the center of the coral was used to represent the iris of the eye. Eyes may have been inserted only on special occasions.

ABOVE LEFT: *The pukao quarry at Puna Pau*

ABOVE RIGHT: *White coral used to make moai eyes*

OPPOSITE: *The moai on Ahu Ko Te Riku at Tahai demonstrates the dramatic effect of coral eyes.*

WOODCARVING

In addition to making huge stone statues, Easter Islanders also carved many smaller wooden figures. These were made from the wood of the *toromiro* tree, a native species now extinct on the island. Many of the carved figures represented the *akuaku*, or spirits of the dead, which were believed to have the power to protect the family who owned them from evil. The most unusual Easter Island carvings, figures with prominent ribs and bulging eyes that make them look like living skeletons, are known as *moai kavakava*. According to legend they represent two ghosts found sleeping in the topknot quarry. The *moai kavakava* were said to possess special powers.

Other Easter Island wood carvings include statues of female figures, paddles, clubs, staffs, lizards, and birdman images. Woodcarving is a craft that continues to be practiced today.

ABOVE: *Carved wooden statue*

LEFT: *Ceremonial carved wooden staffs*

OPPOSITE: *Rongorongo writing. The people of Easter Island are the only known group of Polynesian islanders to have developed a system of writing.*

THE RONGORONGO TABLETS

Among the most mysterious objects found on Easter Island are wooden panels inscribed with rows of what appears to be a kind of writing. The symbols, called *rongorongo*, often take the shape of animals or familiar objects and are believed to be a kind of hieroglyphic picture writing in which each drawing represents a word or idea rather than a letter of the alphabet. On each panel every other line is upside down, so the panel must be turned at the end of each line in order to begin reading the next.

The *rongorongo* symbols are believed to have been guidelines for ceremonial chants. Only the royal family, chiefs, and priests knew their significance. In the late nineteenth century, the last of the high-ranking Easter Islanders died, and the knowledge of the meaning of *rongorongo* disappeared. There are reports of several hundred *rongorongo* tablets seen by missionaries in the nineteenth century, but many of those were apparently lost or destroyed in the chaos of that time. Today there are only twenty-five known examples. Although some general information about the tablets is known, no one has yet broken the *rongorongo* code to know exactly what each symbol means.

THE BIRDMAN COMPETITION

Each September, at the beginning of the Southern Hemisphere spring, flocks of sooty terns, a kind of seabird, come to nest on small rocky islands just off the coast of Easter Island. Both the birds and their eggs were a source of food for the islanders. Since ancient times, there have been ceremonies to celebrate the birds' arrival and to choose an individual known as *tangata manu*, or birdman. The birdman was believed to be the human representative of the creator god Makemake. For the year following the birdman ceremony, he and his family had the right to rule over other families on the island. Although the birdman ceremonies may have occurred in the early centuries of habitation on Easter Island, they became more important in the later years.

The birdman celebration was held at Orongo, the ceremonial village situated on the edge of the crater Rano Kau. After preliminary ceremonies that included feasting and singing, each clan selected a representative, usually an athletic young man, whose job was to swim to the nesting islands, find an egg, return with it unbroken, and present it to his clan leader. The first clan leader to receive an egg became the next birdman.

Birdman competitions were held up to the 1880s. In the final years, however, rule of the birdman and his clan over the other islanders degenerated into cruel and ruthless exploitation of the majority by a few individuals. The birdman competition was discontinued after most islanders were converted to Catholicism by missionaries.

ABOVE: In this rock drawing, two birdman figures, each with a human body and beaked head, face each other.

RIGHT: Birds come to nest annually on three tiny islets that are about a mile offshore from Orongo.

BELOW: Stone houses at the ceremonial site of Orongo. Birdman contestants stayed in the houses before swimming to the nesting islands.

DRAWINGS ON STONE

Another form of artistic expression widely seen on Easter Island is rock art, or petroglyphs—drawings that are either painted on or engraved in rock. Hundreds of images, ranging from birdmen and other religious figures to animals, plants, fish, and human fertility symbols, can be seen at more than a thousand sites on the island. Many of the sites are on rocks near religious centers, while others are inside houses and caves.

One of the richest Easter Island rock art sites is at Orongo, where there are numerous large basalt outcrops covered with carved petroglyphs. Many of the carvings depict birdmen, often holding eggs in their outstretched arms. In some cases the figures overlap one another, because new drawings were engraved on top of older images. It may be that a new birdman drawing was made each year to honor the winning contestant. The creator god, Makemake, is also a frequently drawn image at Orongo and can be recognized by its round face and goggle eyes.

Moai were also sometimes engraved with images. One figure still in the quarry has a picture on its chest of a three-masted ship. Since ancient islanders did not have boats like these, this must have been drawn sometime after the first contact with outsiders.

OPPOSITE ABOVE: This petroglyph, one of hundreds found at Orongo, represents Makemake, the creator god.

OPPOSITE BELOW: Birds carved into the base of Ahu Nau Nau

RIGHT: Moai engraved with three-masted ship

THE END OF PARADISE

About 1680, or perhaps earlier, the quality of life on Easter Island began to diminish, and social organization started to fall apart. At this time, according to tradition, clan rivalries erupted in a bloody battle between the Long Ears and the Short Ears. During the next two hundred years, clan conflict continued to disrupt life on the island. One group would attack another, steal food, kill or kidnap people, and set fire to their property. The victims or their relatives would then retaliate, perpetuating a cycle of attack and revenge. The ultimate insult was to damage another family's *ahu* and *moai*. Moai were pulled down with ropes, and, if possible, the head was broken off at the neck.

Conflict may have grown out of class differences, with lower classes rebelling against increased suppression by the upper classes. Hunger may also have played a part; drought or other weather events may have contributed to famine. Perhaps it was no longer possible to produce enough food to feed the growing number of people on the island. By the end of the seventeenth century, all of the large trees had been cut. Without forests, the land eroded more quickly and retained less moisture, thus making it harder to farm. Also, without wood to build the large oceangoing canoes that were needed for deep-water fishing, people had to rely on the few species of fish that lived close to shore.

The destruction of the island's natural resources undoubtedly contributed to its decline. The disappearance of native plants and wildlife would have occurred slowly, over many generations, and perhaps was barely noticed until it was too late. By then the people had no means to escape their treeless, impoverished land.

Ahu Akahanga. Moai were usually toppled face forward.

AFTER THE ARRIVAL OF EUROPEANS

After Jacob Roggeveen's visit in 1722 it was almost fifty years before outsiders stopped at Easter Island again. A Spanish expedition came in 1770 and was followed four years later by a visit from the Englishman Captain James Cook. Cook traded nails, glass, and other items for food and spent four days exploring the island. He was the first to report that many of the *moai* were knocked down. The *moai* of Easter Island were destroyed gradually, with the last falling sometime in the mid-1800s. By 1864, when missionaries arrived on the island, no *moai* remained standing.

During the nineteenth century, a few more ships stopped briefly, but no one stayed long. Many of the encounters between outsiders and the Rapanui were violent, and there were numerous attempts to capture islanders as slaves.

The worst slave raid occurred in 1862, when more than a thousand Easter Islanders, including the *ariki henua* and all of the *maori*, or learned men, were kidnapped and transported to guano mines in Peru. After the Catholic bishop of Tahiti intervened on their behalf, the Peruvian government agreed to allow them to return home. By that time, however, nearly nine hundred of the men had died of disease or overwork. On the voyage back to Easter Island, most of the rest died of smallpox. The few who survived that ordeal brought the epidemic to the island, where it spread and soon killed all but a few hundred of the inhabitants. Most of them moved away to Tahiti in the 1870s. The Chilean government annexed Easter Island as a territory in 1888 and until 1953 leased most of the land to a sheep-ranching company.

This statue of a kneeling man, known as Tukituri, was discovered in 1955 by members of Thor Heyerdahl's team. Its form is unique among the Easter Island moai and may represent one of the singers at special festivals called riu. In the distance, you can see a stone wall built in the early twentieth century to enclose sheep.

EASTER ISLAND TODAY

Before 1966, when the first airport was built on Easter Island, the only way to get there was by ship, so few visitors came to this remote place. In 1986, the airstrip was greatly enlarged to provide an emergency landing place for the United States space shuttle. Now large jets traveling between Santiago, Chile, and Tahiti stop several times a week. Thousands of people come each year to see the giant statues and to explore what has been called the world's largest open-air museum. For the Rapanui people who live on the island, tourism has brought a renewed pride in their unique heritage and their connections with traditions elsewhere in Polynesia. It has also stimulated a desire for independence and an increased role in local government. About two thousand people live on Easter Island.

As we look at Easter Island today, we see examples of some of humankind's most amazing artistic achievements. We also see the record of some of its darkest moments. Much remains to be learned about Easter Island and the life of its earliest inhabitants. We know that they were mostly farmers and fishermen, and that as they shaped the land to suit their needs they gradually used up many of the island's limited resources. In many ways Easter Island is a model for the world we live in today and is a reminder that natural resources must be used wisely. Continued study of this remote island will help us gain a better understanding of its people and their history, as well as the fascinating story behind the giant "living faces" that line its shores.

AY

Rainbow over Tahai

GLOSSARY

(Note that the singular and plural of Rapanui words are the same. The pronunciation of Rapanui words is phonetic.)

ahu [AH-hoo] a large outdoor altar

akuaku [AH-koo-ah-koo] a supernatural being or spirit of the dead

ana [AH-na] a cave

Anakena [ah-na-KAY-na] A beach on the northeast coast of Easter Island. It is the legendary landing site of the first settlers.

archeologists people who dig up, identify, and sometimes remove evidence of earlier cultures

archeology the study of a prehistoric culture by excavation and analysis of its remains

ariki [ah-REE-kee] men who were believed to possess supernatural powers, which they used to benefit and protect the community

ariki henua [ah-REE-kee HEN-oo-a] the supreme religious leader and the symbol of the island

aringa ora [ah-RIN-ga OR-a] living faces

guano [GWA-no] the manure of seabirds; often used as fertilizer

hare [HA-re] house

hare paenga [HA-re pa-EN-ga] a boat-shaped house with a base of stone and covered with thatch

Hotu Matu'a [HO-too ma-TOO-a] the legendary first *ariki henua* of Easter Island and leader of the original settlers

Makemake [MA-kee-ma-kee] the creator god

maori [MA-o-ree] an honorary title for the master of any craft

midden a mixture of trash with earth and plant matter

moai [MO-aye] a large stone statue

moai kavakava [MO-aye ka-va-KA-va] a wooden statue with prominent ribs

pukao [poo-KA-o] a hatlike stone cylinder mounted on the head of some *moai*, possibly representing a topknot of hair

Puna Pau [POO-na PA-oo] volcanic crater that was the *pukao* quarry

rano [RA-no] a crater lake; also used for the crater in which the lake lies

Rano Raraku [RA-no ra-RA-koo] volcanic crater that was the quarry where most of the Easter Island statues were carved

rongorongo [RON-go-ron-go] an undeciphered picture writing on wooden tablets

taheta [ta-HEE-ta] a stone bowl

tangata manu [tan-GA-ta MA-noo] the birdman; the title given to the winner of the birdman competition

taro [TAR-o] a large, white edible tuber grown for food

Te Pito Te Henua [te PEE to te HEN oo a] navel, or center, of the world; or, possibly, land's end; an ancient name for Easter Island

toki [TO-kee] a stone adze, or ax, used for carving *moai*

toromiro [to-ro-MEE-ro] a small tree whose wood was used for carving on Easter Island

totora [to-TOR-a] a reed that can be used for thatch or weaving

tuff [TUFF] hardened volcanic ash

umu [OO-moo] an earth oven in which food was cooked by means of hot stones

INDEX

Words in the Rapanui language are in *italics*; page numbers in **bold** refer to illustrations.

FOR FURTHER INFORMATION

Books and magazines

Conniff, Richard. "Easter Island Unveiled." *National Geographic*, March
    1993, pp. 54–79.

Diamond, Jared. "Easter's End." *Discover*, August 1995.

Malam, John. *Thor Heyerdahl* (Tell Me About Series). Minneapolis, Minn.:
    Carolrhoda Books, 1999.

Orliac, Catherine, and Michel Orliac. *Easter Island: Mystery of the Stone Giants*.
    Translated from the French by Paul Bahn. New York: Harry N. Abrams, 1995.

Web site

The Easter Island Home Page:

http://www.netaxs.com/ ~ trance/rapanui.html